LEADE

FATHOM BIBLE STUDIES

FATH●M

A DEEP DIVE INTO THE STORY OF GOD

the beginnings
GENESIS

FATHOM: THE BEGINNINGS
GENESIS
LEADER GUIDE

Writer: Charlie Baber
Editor: Ben Howard
Designer: Keely Moore

Websites are constantly changing. Although the websites recommended in this resource were checked at the time this unit was developed, we recommend that you double-check all sites to verify that they are still live and that they are still suitable for students before doing the activity.

ISBN: 9781501837692

PACP10508406-01

17 18 19 20 21 22 23 24 25 26 — 10 9 8 7 6 5 4 3 2 1

MANUFACTURED IN THE UNITED STATES OF AMERICA

CONTENTS

About Fathom

Fathom.

It's such a big word. It feels endless and deep. It's the kind of word that feels like it should only be uttered by James Earl Jones with the bass turned all the way up.

Which means it's the perfect word to talk about a God who's infinite and awe-inspiring. It's also the perfect word for a book like the Bible that's filled with miracles and inspiration, but also wrestles with stories of violence and pain and loss.

The mission of *Fathom* is to dive deep into the story of God that we find in the Bible. You'll encounter Scriptures filled with inspiration and encouragement, and you'll also explore passages that are more complicated and challenging.

Each lesson will focus on one passage, but will also launch into the larger context of how God's story is being told through that passage. More importantly, each lesson will explore how God's story is intimately tied to our own stories, and how a God who is beyond our imagination can also be a God who loves us deeply and personally.

We invite you to wrestle with this and more as we dive deep into God's story.

How to Use This Book

First, we want to thank you for teaching this class! While we strive to provide the best material possible for leaders and students, we know that your personal connection with your teens is the most important part of the lesson.

With that out of the way, welcome to the *Fathom Leader Guide*. Each lesson is designed around Kolb's Learning Cycle and moves students through five sections: *Sync, Tour, Reveal, Build,* and *After.*

Sync introduces the students to the general theme of each lesson with a fun activity. There is both a high-energy and low-energy option to choose from in each lesson. *Tour* is the meat of the lesson and focuses intensely on the central Scripture each week. *Reveal* is a time for reflection where youth can digest the information they've heard and start to make to process it. Then the *Build* section puts this newfound knowledge to practice using creative activities and projects. Finally, *After* gives the students options for practices to try throughout the week to reinforce the central concept of the lesson.

Additionally, before each lesson, a Theology and Commentary section is provided to give you a little more information about the topic being discussed that week.

This Leader Guide is designed to be used hand-in-hand with the *Fathom Student Journal*. Each student will need a journal, and the journals should be kept in the class at the end of the lesson. At the end of the study, give the students their journals as a keepsake to remember what they've learned.

Finally, at the end of this book we've included an Explore More section that offers short outlines for additional lessons if you and your class want to keep diving into these Scriptures after the end of this four-week study.

The Fathom 66 Bible Genre Guide

ENTER ZIP OR LOCATION [   ]

Stories ♡ `TICKETS`
★★★★★
Showtimes: Parts of Genesis, Joshua, Judges, Ruth, 1 Samuel, 2 Samuel, 1 Kings, 2 Kings, 1 Chronicles, 2 Chronicles, Ezra, Nehemiah, Esther, Matthew, Mark, Luke, John, Acts

The Law ♡ `TICKETS`
★★★★★
Showtimes: Parts of Genesis, Exodus, Leviticus, Numbers, Deuteronomy

Wisdom ♡ `TICKETS`
★★★★★
Showtimes: Job, Some Psalms, Proverbs, Ecclesiastes, Song of Solomon, Lamentations, James

Psalms ♡ `TICKETS`
★★★★★
Showtimes: Psalms

The Prophets ♡ `TICKETS`
★★★★★
Showtimes: Isaiah, Jeremiah, Ezekiel, Hosea, Joel, Amos, Obadiah, Jonah, Michah, Nahum, Habakkuk, Zephaniah, Haggai, Zechariah, Malachi

Letters ♡ `TICKETS`
★★★★★
Showtimes: Romans, 1 Corinthians, 2 Corinthians, Galatians, Ephesians, Philippians, Colossians, 1 Thessalonians, 2 Thessalonians, 1 Timothy, 2 Timothy, Titus, Philemon, Hebrews, James, 1 Peter, 2 Peter, 1 John, 2 John, 3 John, Jude

Apocalyptic Writings ♡ `TICKETS`
★★★★★
Showtimes: Daniel, Revelation

The Fathom Bible Storylines

Create   **1**

Invite   **I**

Act   **A**

Redeem   **R**

Experience   **E**

Hope   **H**

Introduction to The Beginnings

Background

The Jewish tradition refers to the first five books of the Bible as *Torah*, the Hebrew word for "law." Genesis, Exodus, Leviticus, Numbers, and Deuteronomy shape the origins of the Israelites in covenant law with Yahweh. As such, they are held in high esteem by the Jewish people, in much the same way that the four Gospels are regarded by Christians. When there is a lack of clarity elsewhere else in the Bible, it is weighed against the Torah for understanding.

You may notice that Genesis feels more like story than law, but the stories of Genesis help situate the covenants God makes first with creation, then with Abraham, and eventually with the Hebrew people collectively.

It was long said that Moses wrote all five books of the Torah, based on a verse at the end of Deuteronomy that reads, "Then Moses wrote this Instruction [Torah] down and gave it to the priests . . . " (31:9). However, it is clear that Genesis, along with the rest of the Torah, was compiled by many different writers over a long period time, and utilizes a variety of literary styles. The Book of Genesis was ultimately brought to its final form by a community who believed that this group of stories told in this particular way was the best introduction to the God of Israel who had made a covenant with the Jewish people.

The title *Genesis* comes from a Greek word and can mean *origin, beginning, generation,* or *descendant.* The first eleven chapters of Genesis tell what is called the Primeval Story, or the origin of all humanity. While these chapters are sparse on what might be considered "law," they are part of the Torah because they mark the beginning stage of humanity's relationship with God and God's covenant promises.

The stories blend together symbolic and historical language in order to foster faith and fidelity to God. For example, in chapter 1, the Hebrew word for man, *adam*, refers to God's creation of all humanity, while in chapter 2, Adam becomes the name of one specific man. This specific man, Adam, both symbolizes the human condition and is understood to be the origin of generations. For the Jewish people, the Primeval Story doesn't just tell us about humanity's origins; it also explains the specific origins of the Hebrew people, tracing their heritage back to Adam, the first man. This is the Torah, the very beginning of God's covenant with God's people.

Fathom Strategy for Reading and Understanding the Bible

"The Bible is written for us, but not to us."

This where we start on our quest. When we read the Bible, we have to constantly remember that the Bible is written for us, but not to us. Understanding the original context of the Bible helps us ask the right questions when interpreting Scripture.

For the first steps in our process, we need to understand how each passage we read functions in context and examine the historical background. When we read a passage, we should ask questions about the era, location, and culture of the original audience, as well as how a particular writing relates to the larger narrative of the Bible. This strategy not only helps us understand a passage's primary meaning, it also gives us guidance on how to translate that meaning into our specific circumstances today.

FATH●M
Creation

Summary

Students will explore how our biblical origin stories show that they are part of God's good creation and made with purpose and hope.

Overview

- **Sync** students with the idea that our origin stories impact our present reality.
- **Tour** through a reflective reading of the Creation story.
- **Reveal** students' deeper thoughts through a prayer-writing exercise.
- **Build** on these thoughts with a caricature drawing and discussion on being made in God's image.
- **After** the lesson, students will choose an activity to remind them about the Creation story this week.

Anchor Point

- Genesis 1:31a—*God saw everything he had made: it was supremely good.*

Supplies

- Student Journals
- Pens or pencils
- Bell or phone alarm
- Dry-erase board or large sheet of blank paper
- Markers
- Pans filled with garden soil
- Baby wipes
- Instrumental background music (optional)

Parent E-mail

This week we begin a four-week study into the opening stories of Genesis. Your kids will learn how the biblical stories of Creation can shape our attitudes and what it means that God declared all Creation good. Here are some thoughts for conversation this week:

- Ask how your family should take a sabbath this week.
- Suggest a time to go out to your child's favorite restaurant to celebrate the goodness of food. Say a prayer over your meal, thanking God for all the hands that prepared the food. While you eat, talk about who was involved in bringing the food from the earth to the table.
- Ask about how your student feels we should take care of the earth. What should we do differently?

Leader Notes

Instead of reading Genesis as a science textbook, the Creation stories are meant to show us that God is the one who crafted order out of chaos. Your teens will be familiar enough with science and history to be suspicious of a literal reading of the Creation stories, but they may not understand how else to read it. Use these stories to expand your students' understanding of God and strengthen their sense of responsibility for others and the created world.

Theology and Commentary

Make time to read Genesis 1:1–2:25 before this lesson.

When God Began to Create

At first glance, the reader might believe the purpose of Genesis 1–2 is to describe *how* God created all things. But the careful reader will notice Genesis 1 tells a very different Creation story from Genesis 2. Genesis 1:1–2:3 organizes Creation into a seven-day structure, with humanity as the culmination of God's creative work. Genesis 2:4-25 shifts the attention from the cosmic scale to the more personal, with God creating Adam before any of the plants or animals. Chapter 1 focuses on the distant, spoken words of *Elohim* (the generic Hebrew word for God), while Genesis 2 gives God the name *Yahweh* (translated LORD God in the CEB), who breathes life into Creation. The differences in logistics indicate the stories may be more about why God created, rather than how.

These stories are meant to go together. Their inconsistencies are held in tension, not in opposition. The interpreter's job is not to decide if humans or plants came first, but to wrestle with the richness of what each story implies for human responsibility in God's creation. While there are plenty of differences between the Creation stories, what they have in common is the clue to how we should understand them.

Both Creation stories share five themes in common: (1) God alone is Creator of all things; (2) all creation has original purpose and goodness; (3) the human relationship to God is unique among those of all creatures; (4) God blesses humanity to take authority over God's creation; (5) humanity is male and female. These similarities shape the core meaning of these stories. Namely, God designed this world for good, and so God continues to care about what happens here. God placed men and women on this earth as God's partners and caretakers of all created things. The Creation stories are placed at the beginning of Torah to mark not just the beginning of history, but the beginning of the themes you'll see through the rest of the Bible.

Future/Past Goodness

Even though the story is universal in its scope, the idea of God separating the waters to bring forth life in Genesis 1 echoes the Exodus story where Moses parts the Reed Sea and the nation of Israel is born. Instead of starting out of violence or random mistakes, God declares creation, and especially humanity, as "supremely good" (1:31). In fact, God makes humanity in God's image and gives them authority to care for creation. This human responsibility is at the heart of God's covenant with Israel. God partners with humanity to bring about ultimate good.

God's creation brings order out of chaos, forms life out of clay, and blesses humanity as the image-bearers of the Creator. While entire books have been written to explain what it means to be made in the image of God, the immediate text implies that, at the least, it means sharing authority to care for all the earth and continuing God's creative act through reproduction. That may be strange to think about with teenagers, but humans having babies, creating new life to carry on the work of creation care, implies hope in the future and a belief that life is worth sharing with others. This is the nature of God, and God has embedded it into the nature of people. As we live into our calling to care for creation and one another, the past moves us toward a supremely good future.

Leader Reflection

I grew up on a chicken farm in rural Virginia and have a vivid memory of the first time I felt really connected to God. My bedroom was the furthest from the wood stove, and I was huddled under fifty pounds of quilts, with my cat sleeping in the nook of my arm. I had an incredible view, acres upon acres of farmland rolling dark blue in the light of the moon. A million stars pierced the night sky, and you could actually see the long arm of the Milky Way stretching from north to south.

I began my nighttime prayers with my eyes open, taking in the wonder of the darkness. As I went through the ritual of asking God to bless Mom and Dad and Great Aunt Maria, it crossed my mind that God made everything I could see outside my window, that God was bigger than the night sky, bigger than the universe, had even existed BEFORE the universe. My seventh-grade mind exploded! I felt exhilarated—God was suddenly so much greater than I had imagined, and somehow I was talking to this infinite, beautiful God.

When have you felt like your view of God expanded? When have you looked out at creation and felt in the depths of your soul, *It is supremely good*? Take a moment to calm your mind, and ask the Holy Spirit to remind you of one of these times in your own life. Try to remember the details. What did you see? What did you hear? As details emerge, lift them up in thanks to God. After several minutes enjoying the goodness of God's creation in prayer, close with this: "Creator, form me. Redeemer, mold me. Sustainer, use me. Amen."

NOTES

SYNC (10 minutes)

High-Energy Option—Superhero Retirement Home

SAY: Think of a superhero. Now, as quickly as possible, tell me the story of how they became a superhero.

[Listen for a few different answers.]

SAY: We all know superhero origin stories, but today we're going to imagine something totally different. What would those superheroes be like in a retirement home?

SAY: I need two to four students who are comfortable being spontaneous. You will be playing a well-known superhero in his or her 90s. You'll all be living together at a superhero retirement home called Comic Convalescence. Anytime an actor begins talking, she must start by saying, "Back in my day. . . . "

SAY: Let's have one volunteer go first. To begin the game, let's take audience suggestions for typical geriatric activities.

[After some good ideas have been shared . . .]

SAY: Now let's take audience suggestions for everyone's favorite superheroes.

[Take five or six suggestions.]

SAY [to the volunteer up front]: Pick the suggestions you like the best, and start the scene without telling anyone which hero you are. Remember, you may be super-old, but you still have use of your super-powers.

SAY [to the other actors]: Once the scene begins, I'll ring the bell to signal the next actor to join the scene as a different superhero. Remember to always start by saying, "Back in my day. . . . " The goal for each actor is to guess the names of the heroes the others are playing and work these into the scene. If you guess wrong, the others can just play it off as memory loss.

[After several minutes of improv, call the scene and applaud your actors.]

ASK: How important is an origin story in shaping the rest of a superhero's life?

SAY: Today we are going to explore the ultimate origin story: God's creation of all things. Let's find out if Genesis helps us understand a little more about ourselves.

Low-Energy Option—Crowd-Sourced Origins

SAY: We all know that life had to start somewhere. Before we dive into the lesson, let's put together what we know about the story of how the universe began. Try to remember what ideas you know from the Bible and what you know from science; it's okay if you don't know the exact details. As each person shares, we'll alternate between ideas from science and ideas from the Bible. So if one person shares something about the Big Bang Theory, the next person should share something about Genesis, and back-and-forth. If you think of a question instead of a fact, you can say that as well, and we'll write it down.

[Ask a volunteer to write the answers down on a dry-erase board or a large piece of paper. Let the students lead the discussion, and only offer input to keep the momentum going. The goal is to see where everyone stands before digging into the Scripture.]

ASK: What do you make of these differences? Do you think science and faith can go together?

SAY: Today we are going to explore God's creation of all things. Let's find out if Genesis helps us understand a little more about ourselves.

TOUR (15-20 minutes)

[It's ideal to hold this activity in a church garden if you have one. Otherwise, pass around a few baking pans that you've filled with soil. Make sure you have wipes to clean hands after you're done.]

SAY: Let's get two students to read us the first story of Creation in Genesis 1. While they read, everyone else run your fingers through the soil and form it into shapes to help you imagine what you're hearing. As you listen, ask yourself, *Why is God creating? Why is God giving authority over creation to people? Why is God resting on the seventh day?*

[Students read Genesis 1:1–2:3 from the Student Journal.]

ASK:
- Why do you think God created?
- Why do you think God gave authority over creation to humanity?
- Why do you think God rested on the seventh day?

SAY: The Bible begins with the most expansive view of God anyone can imagine. Genesis 1 tells us that God exists before the universe, even before time. God simply speaks an idea and BANG! it happens. Just think about what you know about the universe, how it continues to expand, how all the life we know of is confined to this one planet that is just a speck in a massive galaxy, and how that galaxy is just a speck among countless other galaxies. God is bigger than all of that, yet God got so close as to design the tiniest atomic particles that come together to make us who we are.

ASK: This Scripture demonstrates that God has ordered all of creation. Relatedly, science seeks to understand the order of all things. How do you think understanding more about science might help you appreciate God's creation more?

SAY: Faith is key when Scripture claims that God made you in God's image. You can't prove scientifically that you're an image-bearer of God, but God gave you the ability and responsibility to take charge of and care for the universe God created. You're called to care for other people and to care for other living creatures. Plants, the land and water, and the atmosphere are all your responsibility. God made everyone else in the image of God too. Maybe you prefer to call this human dignity, but there's something built into us that respects and cares for others. That's a huge responsibility because, in case you haven't noticed, the world has a lot of problems these days.

ASK: How do you interpret the Scripture where God says to humanity: "Fill the earth and master it. Take charge"? What does it mean for humanity to take charge of creation?

SAY: This Creation story ends with a day of rest. Sabbath is supposed to be a day to enjoy all that God has created. It's supposed to be a break from the normal routine to remind us that for all our responsibilities, God is still ultimately the one in charge.

ASK: Why do you think Scripture includes a day of rest in this Creation story?

[Now might be a good time to share a personal testimony. If you read the Leader Reflection, share briefly about a time your view of God expanded, and how that made a difference in the way you lived your life.]

REVEAL (10 minutes)

SAY: Take the next five minutes to pray with your pen in your Student Journals. Try to write complete thoughts, and never erase or scratch out anything. As you write, pray the words in your mind to God. It doesn't have to be perfect. It doesn't have to make sense to anyone else. Pray about something you learned today that you hadn't thought about before, or pray about all the questions you have after today's lesson. Afterward, you'll have a few minutes to share your thoughts with others.

Journal Prompt
• When I think about why God created all things . . .

[Allow students time to write. If your group struggles with silence, have instrumental music playing during this time. A few minutes into their time, prompt them with the following.]

SAY: If you get stuck, rewrite your last thought until something new comes to you.

[Have the students gather in groups of three and share what they wrote.]

ASK: Did any of you write about similar topics? What themes kept coming up in your prayers?

BUILD (10 minutes)

It's All Good

SAY: Pair up with someone who was NOT in your group during the Reveal activity. Swap Student Journals with your partner and turn to the Build page. In the space provided, draw a picture of your partner in their book. While you draw, both of you should discuss the following questions:

- How does your partner bear the image of God? Around the picture you're drawing, write down the things you say.
- What difference does it make to you to know that you are a hand-crafted image-bearer of God?

[Give the students eight minutes to draw and write down their answers.]

SAY: Okay, now return the books to their rightful owners. Look at the drawing your partner made of you. Look at the words written down to remind you how you are an image-bearer of God.

ASK: Which do you like better: your partner's drawing or the words that describe you? Why?

[Allow for responses.]

ASK: God says of all creation, "It is supremely good." What difference does it make to believe that not just you but all things were created with a good purpose?

AFTER (5 minutes)

[Invite the students to participate in an After activity. Send them a reminder during the week.]

Social Media Project: #Godwatchers

SAY: Plan to post one daily picture celebrating one aspect of God's creation, with the hashtags *#itsallgood #Godwatchers*. If you don't know where to start, post about each day of Creation. (Today, post an artsy photo of light; tomorrow, of the sky; the next day, of water meeting the land; and so on.) Next week when we come back together, we'll look through all the pics everyone shared.

Sabbath Keepers

SAY: Talk to your family about a way to enjoy the sabbath together. Think about something all of you enjoy, and offer to help your family prepare so that everyone can actually have a day of rest.

Creation Care

SAY: This is a great week to think about how many of God's resources we waste. Every time you throw something in the trash, from food to wrappers, say this prayer: "Creator God, show me how to better care for your world." When you come to our next meeting, share a way you have reduced the amount of things you waste.

PRAYER

SAY: Think of one thing God created that you are thankful for. Share it out loud when we come to that part of the prayer.

Creator God, thank you for all good things. Thank you for creating us with purpose and hope. We especially want to thank you for . . .

[Students share their thanks out loud.]

Help us this week to care for one another and for the world you created. In Jesus' name. Amen.

FATH●M
Fall

Summary

Students will investigate the escalating impact of sin on their relationships with God, one another, and creation. Sin is bigger than we realize, but God's grace is always ready to make things right again.

Overview

- **Sync** with the idea that small actions can have big consequences.
- **Tour** through a dramatic reading of Genesis 3 and 4.
- **Reveal** deeper connections to Scripture by recalling consequences we've experienced for our own actions.
- **Build** on these concepts by writing prayers for one another to avoid temptation.
- **After** the lesson, students will apply these ideas through activities that will remind them about core themes throughout the week.

Anchor Point

- Genesis 3:10—*I heard your sound in the garden; I was afraid because I was naked, and I hid myself.*

Supplies

- Student Journals
- Pens or pencils
- Washable markers
- Fruit and fruit snacks (in a bowl labeled "Forbidden Fruit")
- Instrumental background music (optional)

Parent E-mail

This week our students will explore the topic of sin. They will learn how mistrust in God leads to shame, blame, and distance, and they will be challenged to consider the ways sin impacts our relationships with God, one another, and creation. We'll also explore how God responds to our sin with grace, but also with consequences. Here are some ways to engage this week:

- Talk to your child about your own responses to their misbehavior and how that shapes the way they learn.
- Share a story from the news or from pop culture where one person's misbehavior affected many other people. Ask your child to share a similar story. Ask them if these people intended to hurt so many others with their actions. What do they think the appropriate consequences would be?

Leader Notes

Students have a strong sense of fairness and are starting to notice the realities of sin and brokenness in the world around them. These early Genesis stories about sin and consequences should resonate with them as they begin to understand how isolated actions can spiral into larger problems. As you move through these stories, remember to remind them that God's grace is always ready to make things right again. By internalizing these ideas, they can become more thoughtful about their own actions and more honest when dealing with their own failures.

Theology and Commentary

Make time to read Genesis 3:1–4:16 before reading the commentary below.

Sin From the Outside In

The opening stories of Genesis show us a downward spiral from the supreme goodness of God's Creation to a time when "humanity had become thoroughly evil on the earth and . . . every idea their minds thought up was always completely evil" (6:5). Gerhard Von Rad calls this the "avalanche of sin," but notes that God's grace continued to grow and abound with each increasing sin and consequence. When Adam and Eve took the forbidden fruit and became ashamed of their nakedness, God clothed and protected them even after expelling them from the garden of Eden. After Cain murdered his brother and feared for his own life, God protected him from retribution even as Cain was cursed to wander forever. Von Rad describes these Genesis stories as "a story of God with man, the story of continuously new punishment and at the same time gracious preservation."[1]

But if God created all things "supremely good," where does sin come from? Genesis 3 tells the story of a talking snake, "the most intelligent of all the wild animals that the Lord God had made" (3:1). This outside force poses a challenge to Adam and Eve, to take God's word for it or to test God's word and discover either great reward (gain the knowledge of gods) or severe consequence (death). Adam and Eve choose to trust the voice of the snake more than the word of the Lord, and this choice immediately changes their experience. Adam and Eve see their nakedness, and what was once a supremely good gift of God is now a source of shame. When confronted about their behavior, no one takes responsibility. While Scripture does not blatantly call anything a sin in this story, we discover that choices, especially choosing an alternative to God's plan, can have consequences bigger than anyone realized.

---

1. Gerhard Von Rad, *Genesis: A Commentary*, OTL (London: SCM Press, 1972), 153.

In the story of Cain, sin is portrayed as a prowling animal looking for the opportunity to attack its prey. Just as the Lord commanded Adam and Eve to rule over the animals of the earth, now God gives Cain a choice: Rule over sin, or you will let sin rule over you. The text gives no reason why God prefers Abel's sacrifice over Cain's, and the reason is unimportant. The story is about jealousy. When one person has what another does not, what is the appropriate human response? God knows Cain's internal crisis, God cares about what Cain will do next, but God gives Cain freedom to take the next step.

In the end, Cain lets sin rule him and he murders his brother. As with Adam and Eve, there is nowhere Cain can hide from God. While his parents were filled with shame, Cain is filled with fear of the consequences of his actions.

Cain is cursed to be a nomad, but God also places a mark on Cain to protect him from harm. This is reminiscent of the Passover story, where the lamb's blood causes the angel of death to pass by and spare the homes of the Hebrews. In the Christian tradition of baptism, the sign of the cross is made on the forehead of the believer as a symbol of God's presence in that person's life. The mark of Cain also is a symbol that God is with Cain despite his sin. Through God's grace, the cycle of violence would come to an end. Cain would spend his life wandering after the murder of his brother, but the mark of God's presence would always be with him.

Leader Reflection

Can you remember a time in your teenage years when your sin felt so much bigger than you? For one student, this moment will come when she realizes that the words she's said about someone else have spread beyond her control, and what felt like a funny joke has now devastated another person. For another student, he'll realize this the first time he looks at pornography and finds himself confused about a mixture of shame with the desire for more.

On the surface, your group may joke about serious issues, but there is always, ALWAYS, a deeper place in each of us that knows the depth of our sins. Joking and nonchalance are standard ways we protect ourselves from consequences and accepting culpability for our actions.

Take a moment to pray for your students and the lesson you're teaching this week. As you pray, ask God to reveal a time in your life when you experienced tremendous grace in response to your sin.

Pray for your students slowly, by name. If you know the sins they struggle with, pray for their perseverance. If you don't know, trust that God knows. Pray for the mark of God's grace to be with them and that they will move into the fullness of the life God desires for them.

NOTES

SYNC (5-10 minutes)

High-Energy Option—Group Truth or Consequences

SAY: One action can lead to many unexpected consequences. Let's play a game of "Truth or Consequences" with a twist. I'm going to divide our room in half. Each round, I'll call a contestant from each team forward and I'll ask them each a trivia question. If you give the correct answer, your team gets five points. However, if you give the wrong answer, your entire team has to suffer the consequence while you watch. If your entire team acts out the consequence, your team wins three points. If they don't, your team loses three points.

[Play three rounds, but watch your time. This should be fun. Don't make anyone do anything they aren't comfortable doing!]

SAY: Let's start Round One. Here's the consequence for either contestant getting it wrong: You must watch as your teammates sing the entire chorus of a song of their choice.

Here's the question for Team ONE: What artist has the most number one hits? *[Answer: The Beatles.]*

Okay, Team TWO's question: What is the best-selling album of all time? *[Answer: Thriller by Michael Jackson.]*

[After both teams have answered, administer the consequence and award points.]

SAY: Let's get two new contestants. Here's the consequence for giving the wrong answer: You must watch as your entire team removes their shoes and smells one another's feet.

Team ONE's question: How many bones are in the typical adult foot? *[Answer: 26.]*

Team TWO, here's your question: *Tinea pedis* is the scientific name for what fungal infection? *[Answer: Athlete's foot.]*

[After both teams have answered, administer the consequence and award points.]

SAY: Next contestants, please! If you give the wrong answer this round, you must watch as your entire team uses a marker to draw facial hair on one another. *[Use WASHABLE markers for this one!]*

Team ONE's question: In a deck of cards, which suit is the only one where the king has no mustache? *[Answer: Hearts.]*

Team TWO's question: The average male beard has approximately how many whiskers growing in it? (A) 3,000; (B) 30,000; (C) 300,000; (D) 3,000,000 *[Answer: (B) 30,000.]*

[After both teams have answered, administer the consequence, award points, and declare a winner. Give the winning team the fruit snacks from the Forbidden Fruit bowl.]

SAY: Sometimes one person's actions can have major unintended consequences! Last week we learned that God made everything "supremely good" and that everyone is made in the image of God. We also learned that sabbath rest gives us hope for a future where all things enjoy God's presence. Today, let's explore what went wrong.

Low-Energy Option—Snowballing Consequences, Round-Robin Story

SAY: One action can lead to many unexpected consequences. Let's create a round-robin story together. I need one volunteer to stand in the middle and act out the story as we make it up. Going in order, each person around the class will add a new sentence to continue the story. The first time around the room, focus on setting up the character and some kind of bad action the character does.

[Go around the room the first time. Don't let people describe consequences yet.]

SAY: That was good! Now this time when we go around the room, let's focus on describing the consequences of what the character did. Each consequence should be worse than the previous one.

[Go around the room a second time.]

SAY: This time when we go around the room, describe a resolution to the story. It can be a happy ending or a terrible ending. Let's go!

[Go around the room the last time.]

SAY: Let's have a round of applause for our actor and for all of our storytellers! Last week we learned that God made everything "supremely good," and that everyone is made in the image of God. We also learned that sabbath rest gives us hope for a future where all things enjoy God's presence. Today, let's explore what went wrong.

TOUR (15-20 minutes)

The Origins of Sin

SAY: We're going to take a look at the origins of sin in Genesis. First, let's divide into two groups. Group One will read a story from Genesis 3:1-13, and Group Two will read a story from Genesis 4:1-16. Each group will read through their story (found in your Student Journals), assign parts, and then act it out for the rest of the class. You'll need a narrator to read the story while the other students act it out. Take a few minutes to get organized.

[Give both groups a few minutes to get ready, and then have both groups perform.]

SAY: When we talk about the origins of sin, most people talk about Adam and Eve eating an apple. After hearing these two stories, what do you think the first sin was?

[After each answer, push back by asking, "Are you sure?"]

SAY: Did anyone notice the word *sin* anywhere in these stories? It's not there until Genesis 4:7! But the story clearly begins with a question that leads to an action that leads to negative consequences. Help me break that down:

- **What's the question in Genesis 3:1 that starts this whole process?** *"Did God really say . . . ?"*

- **What actions played out in response to the question?** *Eve repeated God's rule, the serpent corrected her, Adam and Eve took the forbidden fruit and ate it. (Stop them there.)*

- **What negative consequences happened immediately as a result of those actions?** *They became ashamed of their nakedness and tried to cover up, they hid from God, they passed the blame for their actions.*

SAY: Eating some fruit seems pretty harmless, and you wouldn't be the first person to wonder why the actions of Adam and Eve are such a big deal. Even though the Bible doesn't call this a sin, there's a clear movement from losing trust in God to actions demonstrating a mistrust in God to shame, blame, and distance. Sin is bigger than we realize, but God's grace is always ready to make things right again.

ASK:
- Look at the Scripture text your group acted out. How did the sin in the story damage the sinner's relationship with God?
- How did the sin in the story create distance between the people involved?
- Did the sin in the story affect the rest of creation in any way?

REVEAL (10 minutes)

SAY: Take the next five minutes to reflect in your journals about a time you were punished by your parents or a teacher for something you did wrong. How did you feel when you were caught? How did you respond to the punishment? Were they fair in the way they responded to you? What grace, if any, did you receive during this experience? How did this experience shape you to do things differently the next time?

[Give the students five minutes to write their answers. If your group struggles with silence, have instrumental music playing quietly in the background.]

SAY: Break up into groups of three and share what you wrote with the other members of the group. Pay attention to the similarities and differences in your experiences.

[Allow another five minutes for students to share and discuss their stories with one another.]

BUILD (10 minutes)

ASK: In the aftermath of Adam, Eve, and Cain, sin began to be an increasingly large problem. By Genesis 6:11, the writer of Genesis says that "the earth had become corrupt and was filled with violence." Do you believe sin is completely isolated, or do you think sin can be contagious, spreading from one person to the next?

[Allow for two or three answers. Then, put a chair in the middle of the room with enough space for everyone to stand around it.]

SAY: In Genesis 4, sin is described as a prowling beast ready to bring down Cain. Sometimes we feel powerless against the temptations we face, but we're never alone. Right now, we're going to create prayers of blessing to pray for one another. Take a few minutes to write your prayer in your journal. When you're finished, we're going to pray the prayers we wrote on behalf of one another.

[Give the students five minutes to create their prayers.]

SAY: We're going to take turns now praying for one another in the Prayer Chair. When one person sits in the chair, the rest of us will put our hands on that person's head or shoulders. One of you will make the sign of the cross on that person's forehead with your finger and say the prayer you just wrote in your journal. After the prayer, we'll all say "Amen," the person in the chair will get up, and the person who just prayed over the person in the chair will sit in the chair. We'll keep going until everyone has been prayed for.

[Tip: The teacher should do the prayer first to demonstrate for the class.]

ASK: How did it feel to be prayed for in this way?

AFTER (5 minutes)

[Invite the students to participate in an After activity. Send them a reminder during the week.]

Social Media Project: #Godwatchers

SAY: This week post one daily picture displaying the brokenness of creation with the tagline *#HowLongOLord #Godwatchers*. Next week when we come together, we'll share the pictures everyone posted as we begin class.

Crouching at Your Door

SAY: God warned Cain that sin was crouching at his door like a prowling beast. This week look up 1 Corinthians 10:13, which talks about this kind of temptation, and write it down on an index card. Put the index card somewhere you'll see it regularly as a reminder to pray that God will help you to overcome temptation.

Push Notification Prayer

SAY: This week you're going to be assigned a prayer partner. During the week, send your prayer partner a text to let him or her know they're not alone when facing temptation. You can use the prayer you wrote in the Build section or you can write a new prayer. If you need prayer during the week, send your prayer partner a note saying, "Pray for me."

PRAYER

SAY: Join me in our closing prayer, found in your journal.

God of grace,
Thank you for always giving us the chance
To choose to do what's right.
Forgive us when we fail.
Strengthen us to forgive when others fail us.
Help us to trust you through every temptation,
In the strength and power of Jesus Christ. Amen.

FATH●M
Flooded

Summary

In the story of the Flood, we learn that God is deeply moved by the actions of humanity. In the aftermath of the Flood, we see how God self-limits and keeps the promises made with creation.

Overview

- **Sync** with the question of where God is during disasters.
- **Tour** through an experiential reading of the Flood story.
- **Reveal** students' thoughts about the connection between God and suffering.
- **Build** understanding about how we can work together with God to help end suffering and injustice.
- **After** the lesson, students will reinforce these ideas through activities that remind them about God's promises.

Anchor Point

- Genesis 9:15b-16—*Floodwaters will never again destroy all creatures. The bow will be in the clouds, and upon seeing it I will remember the enduring covenant between God and every living being of all the earth's creatures.*

Supplies

- Student Journals
- Pens or pencils
- Index cards
- Dry-erase board or a large piece of paper
- Bulletin board with pins
- 10–15 headlines that portray stories of violence in the world
- Glasses of water
- Small mirrors that fit in water glasses
- Flashlights
- Blue and red fingerpaint
- Wipes to clean fingers after painting
- Tape
- Candy that comes in purple, orange, red, yellow, and green colors (one pack per three students)

Parent E-mail

This week we're studying the story of the Flood. We'll discuss how God is motivated to send the Flood by the violence and injustice of humanity, and we'll wrestle with the idea of a God who is deeply troubled by evil but has promised not to intervene by wiping out all the "bad" people.

As you talk with your child this week, think about how you have come to terms with a loving God in a world filled with bad things. You don't need solid answers. Sometimes, just discussing this question openly frees your teen to dig deeper into her or his own faith.

Leader Notes

Your students have probably wondered why a good God allows bad things to happen. Whether they've experienced personal loss or just paid attention to the bad stuff in the news, they will likely not be satisfied by quick, thoughtless answers. Use this lesson as a way to explore how God is deeply concerned with the violence and evils perpetrated by humanity. Help your students consider what it means that God limits the use of God's own power to intervene.

Theology and Commentary

Be sure to read Genesis 6:5-13 and Genesis 9:1-17 before you read this section.

The Broken Heart of God

If your students are paying attention to the story, they may be troubled by the image of a flood destroying every living thing that wasn't on that boat. Many people question their faith when faced with what insurance companies call "acts of God." It's even more dismaying to read a story indicating that God *really was* the cause of such a natural disaster.

So who is this God that would send a flood to destroy the entire world? In this story, we discover a God who sees, who regrets, and who is heartbroken (6:5-6). These words indicate that God's intentions for humanity in the Creation stories have been deeply betrayed.

This is a complicated story. Far from the idea of a distant, immovable God, we're shown a God who has a deep emotional connection to creation. Far from the idea of a timeless, omniscient deity, God is said to regret making humanity. Adding to the messiness, God is so horrified with human violence that God decides the best solution is to use violence to destroy everything (save the few on the ark).

Ultimately, this is a story of judgment and grace, of destruction and promise. This story brings together many of the feelings and questions we often have in times of tragedy, and yet leaves those questions largely unanswered. As you prepare to teach, you will want to wrestle with what it means that God is deeply moved by the actions of humanity and is a God who keeps promises.

Leader Reflection

I've been on two mission trips to the Gulf Coast. The first was to New Orleans before anyone had ever heard of Hurricane Katrina. The second trip was a trip to the coast of Mississippi about a year after the hurricane hit and claimed the lives of nearly two thousand people and left over $108 billion in property damage. It's hard to imagine the devastation of a natural disaster until you go to the scene, see the rubble, and talk to the people who lost loved ones.

In the film *Hotel Rwanda,* which documents the Rwandan genocide, there's a line that continues to haunt me. While filming the atrocities, a journalist turns to a colleague and says, "I think if people see this footage, they'll say, 'Oh my God, that's horrible,' and then go on eating their dinners." I am guilty of that reaction to most bad news in the world, and I am guilty of that reaction when I read the story of the Flood. My heart is broken for a moment, and then I go on with my life, sheltering myself with comfort to avoid the pain of the world. What else can we do?

The story of the Flood portrays a God who does not simply go on eating dinner. God is deeply heartbroken by the violence of the world.

Spend five minutes in prayer for your students, some of whom might already be wrestling with these questions. Lift up those people you know who are grieving from loss or illness. Pray for the promise of God's faithfulness to become a source of encouragement for all who suffer now.

NOTES

SYNC (5-10 minutes)

High-Energy Option—Reverse Charades

[Before class, create a stack of index cards with Noah-themed clues. Here are some suggestions: PIG, FLOOD, GIRAFFE, ARK, LION, NOAH, GOD, DOVE, RAIN, RAINBOW, OLIVE BRANCH, PANDA, COW, ELEPHANT, EVIL, MOUNTAIN, KANGAROO.]

SAY: First, split up into two teams. We're going to play "Reverse Charades." Pick one person to come forward for your team. I will hold up a card so that everyone can see it, EXCEPT for the player at the front. The entire team has to act out the card, and the player at the front has to guess what's on the card. Your team can make noises and give hints, but they can't say any part of the word on the card or say what it rhymes with. Each player will have thirty seconds to try and guess the word on the card. Each correct guess is a point for your team.

All the cards are somehow connected to today's story about Noah. Let's go!

[Play as many rounds as you can in the time allotted.]

SAY: Last week we learned how sin creates distance in the relationships between God, humanity, and creation. Today we're going to explore the story of Noah and consider together what's going on with God when bad things happen.

Low-Energy Option—When Bad Things Happen

SAY: I need two volunteers. Together you're going to write down all the things we brainstorm together as a class.

We're all familiar with the story of Noah and the Flood. However, did you know that almost every culture has some sort of flood story where the world is wiped out by water? Before we dive into the Scripture, I want everyone's help brainstorming other disaster stories from the Bible or history or even fiction. It's okay if you don't know exact details.

[Give the students five minutes to brainstorm whatever comes to mind.]

SAY: All of those are remote; can you think of some disasters that you've experienced? Maybe you've witnessed a flood or a tornado. Add that to the list.

[Give the students another minute or two to brainstorm ideas.]

SAY: Today, we're going to explore the story of Noah and consider together what's going on with God when bad things happen.

TOUR (15-20 minutes)

[Before class begins, set up a bulletin board with 10–15 headlines or stories about violence. Use caution not to show gory or bloody images. At the center of your bulletin board, print Genesis 6:5-6. Also fill several glasses with water and place them on a table. Inside of each glass of water, place a small mirror at an angle. You will need flashlights at the table as well.]

SAY: Most of us have grown up hearing the story of Noah and the huge boat he builds and fills with every kind of animal to save them from a massive flood. Today we're going to direct our focus on what this story teaches us about the character of God.

[Direct the students to the wall of headlines.]

SAY: On the wall, you'll see a lot of stories about bad things that have happened around the world. We have learned that God made all things supremely good, but humanity has resisted God. Last week we looked at the ways that sin is bigger than we realize. Many people see the sin in the world and think God is distant or unconcerned, but that isn't the case.

[Ask a student to read Genesis 6:5-6 aloud from the middle of the wall.]

SAY: Look at the wall and find a headline that breaks your heart. Dip your finger in blue fingerpaint and spread the paint over one of the headlines as you read it out loud. After each person reads a headline, we'll all say this simple prayer: **"How long, O Lord?"**

[Let each student paint over one of the headlines with the fingerpaint as the group repeats the prayer.]

SAY: I need a volunteer to dip a finger in the red fingerpaint and draw a heart over each of the following phrases as I point them out: "The LORD saw"; "The LORD regretted"; "He was heartbroken."

[Have the volunteer stand at the wall while you read the following.]

SAY: God sees the evil that happens, so God must continue to be interested in what God created.

[Point to "The Lord saw."]

SAY: If God regrets making humanity here, Scripture suggests that God was somehow surprised that things didn't go the way God intended.

[Point to "The Lord regretted."]

SAY: God's heart breaks because God loves God's creation and is invested in humanity.

[Point to "He was heartbroken."]

SAY: Once the paint is dry, take the headline you painted over off the wall and tape it into your Student Journal as a reminder.

[Direct students to the table with the water glasses.]

SAY: Let's read a little bit more of the Flood story. I need a volunteer to read Genesis 7:1-4 aloud.

[Let a student read the verses aloud.]

SAY: The Flood wipes out most of God's creation. It is both the consequence of all the violence and injustice in the world, and a chance for God and the world to start over. The Flood story is often associated with baptism, where the water is a symbol of death to sin and rebirth in Jesus Christ.

SAY: In the Flood story, the rainbow is the symbol of a new covenant between God and creation. We're going to try and make our own rainbows right now. Use one of the lights on the table to shine into the mirror until you see a rainbow form from the angle. Adjust the mirror or your light until you see those colors refract. I'm going to turn the lights out to pitch black on the count of three. One, two, three.

[Turn out lights.]

SAY: I need two volunteers to use their flashlights to read from Genesis 9 while you make your rainbows.

[Have the first volunteer read Genesis 9:5-11 and the second read Genesis 9:14-16. After these verses are read, turn the lights back on.]

SAY: This story is kind of like Creation 2.0. In this new creation, God sets limits on humanity and for the first time in Scripture says that the penalty for murder is death. But in this new creation, God also sets limits on God's own use of power to deal with our sin. Never again will God use natural disasters to punish people for sin. The rainbow is a symbol that God sees our sin and our pain, that God is heartbroken over us, and that God remembers and keeps God's promises to us.

REVEAL (10 minutes)

Taste the Rainbow

SAY: Split into groups of two or three, and grab a pack of candy to share. Each color represents a different emotion. Look in your Student Journal and grab the color of candy that best represents your feelings about God and the story of the Flood.

- Purple—Deep thoughts or sorrow
- Orange—Peace or balance
- Red—Passion or anger
- Yellow—Light or joy
- Green—Growth or development

Journal Prompt

The rainbow is a symbol of the promise that God will not flood the earth again. When I think about God's role in the Flood story, I feel . . .

[Give the students five minutes to journal.]

SAY: Share your answer with your group and tell how the color of candy you chose connects to that answer. Also, you can eat your candy now.

[Allow the students to share with one another for five minutes.]

BUILD (10 minutes)

New Creation World-Leader Summit

SAY: Turn to the Build section of your Student Journal. Think out loud with me. What are problems in the world that might cause God to be heartbroken?

[Allow everyone to give an answer.]

SAY: Using the same groups from the Reveal section, I'm going to assign you one of the problems we just named.

[Assign each group one of the issues from the brainstorming time.]

SAY: Take a few moments to think together how your team can lead the human race to put an end to this particular injustice without violence. When I call us back together, each group will send forth a leader to our New Creation World-Leader Summit. The leaders will create a panel, each briefly explaining his or her group's problem and how they propose to fix it.

[Allow time for groups to discuss.]

SAY: The New Creation World-Leader Summit will begin in thirty seconds. World leaders, take your places!

[Allow representatives to gather at the front of the room.]

SAY: I call this meeting to order! World leaders, share your issue and your proposed solution.

[After all leaders have spoken, address the audience].

SAY to the audience: We are now going to vote on which proposal you think is most likely to work. I will stand behind each group leader, one at a time, and you will vote with your applause. The group with the loudest applause wins.

[Stand behind each student one by one, listening for the applause. If it's close, go back and forth between the two you think have the loudest applause, then make up your mind and announce the winner.]

ASK the winner: How many years do you think it will take for your proposal to completely end this problem?

[Allow for a response.]

ASK everyone: Are you willing to wait that long? Would you rather God violently intervene to stop human injustice or would you rather God give humans strength to make a difference because God suffers with us? Why?

[Allow for a variety of responses. Push back by asking, "Are you sure?" after each response.]

ASK: Christians have long associated our baptism with the story of Noah and the Flood. How might what you've learned today strengthen you to take your baptism more seriously in an effort to make the world a better place?

AFTER (5 minutes)

[Invite the students to participate in an After activity. Send them a reminder during the week.]

Social Media Project: #Godwatchers

SAY: Post one picture of water every day with the tagline *#flooded #Godwatchers.* Each day, find a creative new use for water that reminds you of God's promises or of the new creation. Next week when we come back together, we'll share the pictures everyone posted.

Clearasil Christians

SAY: It is said that Martin Luther would routinely wash his face and remind himself, "I am baptized." This simple practice was a regular reminder that he was created new in Christ. This week when you clean your face, say, "I am baptized." Think about what that means and let it lead you to make this world a little better each day.

Rainbow Hunters

SAY: There are plenty of problems in the world, and none of us can fix everything. But we can have an effect on the things we care about the most. This week, think about one issue that really bothers you, and learn more about it. Look for organizations that are seeking to put an end to that type of injustice. Learn about small things you can do to be part of the solution . . . then do something.

PRAYER

SAY: Join me in the prayer printed in your Student Journal.

Heartbroken God,
Break our hearts for what breaks yours,
Open our eyes to injustice,
Forgive us when we are part of the problem,
Transform us to be part of the solution,
Through our baptism and the power of Christ. Amen.

FATH●M
Scattered

Summary

Human diversity is an important part of God's plan. The Tower of Babel helps us explore how unity and separation are both integral to God's plan for the world.

Overview

- **Sync** with a game that challenges students to communicate with one another without using the same language.
- **Tour** Genesis 11 by praying through the Scripture and then empowering students to discover and teach the Scripture themselves.
- **Reveal** a time in your own life when you worked with a large group of people to do either good or harm.
- **Build** on these ideas through an activity where students translate poems of thanks into other languages.
- **After** the lesson, challenge students to take on an activity this week that will push them to be open to people of different cultures.

Anchor Point

- Genesis 11:9—*Therefore, it is named Babel, because there the L*ORD *mixed up the language of all the earth; and from there the L*ORD *dispersed them over all the earth.*

Supplies

- Student Journals
- Pens or pencils
- One box of uncooked spaghetti noodles for every four students
- Three to four bags of mini-marshmallows, small gumdrops, or jelly beans
- Large bowl
- Inflatable balloon
- At least ten Legos (or other similar brick-building toy) for each person in class
- At least one computer or mobile device connected to the Internet
- Instrumental background music (optional)

Parent E-mail

We are studying the Tower of Babel in Genesis 11 this week, from which we will learn that human diversity is an important part of God's plan. Prejudice and racism are uncomfortable topics, but these are critical conversations to have with your teenager. Here are some conversation starters to use with your child this week:

- Talk about biases you learned as a teenager or that you've come across in your adult life. Ask your child what biases she or he has encountered.
- Talk about positive experiences you've had with someone of a different race, language, or religion. Invite your child to share his or her experiences.

Leader Notes

Your students may already have strong opinions about people of different races and languages, yet they will likely not see this as prejudice. It is likely that your students will have experienced some sort of racial stereotyping. As you study the story of the Tower of Babel, help them evaluate what is positive about cultural variety and notice ways we harm one another when we devalue people who are different from us.

Theology and Commentary

Make time to read Genesis 10:1–11:9 before the lesson this week.

As we come to Genesis 10 and 11, the narrative moves from the history of the world to the history of the particular group of people who will become the nation of Israel. The Tower of Babel is the hinge between these two histories. It is a story about a particular place, called Babel (which means *confusion*), but it is also meant to explain the universal reality of different languages and cultures.

Chapter 10 is often called the Table of Nations, as it describes the descendants of Noah as the founders of all the nations, cultures, and languages known at the time Genesis was written. It's surprising, then, that after thirty-two verses explaining where all the cultures and languages come from, Genesis 11:1 begins with, "All people on the earth had one language and the same words." Much like the Creation stories in Genesis 1 and 2, chapters 10 and 11 shouldn't be read chronologically. The first chapter tells the tale from a cosmic viewpoint, while the second chapter retells the story up close. The details are different, but the message is the same.

In chapter 11, a group of people with a common language decide to settle down and build a city with a tower to the sky. Their purpose is made plain: "Let's make a name for ourselves so that we won't be dispersed over all the earth" (11:4). The Lord judges this negatively, and creates different languages for the people, dispersing them "over all the earth" (11:8). This story is an example of what's taking place in chapter 10. It's common for people with the same language and culture to hunker down into a tight-knit community, but God appears to look negatively on the community that refuses diversification.